The Echo Within

"In this so-beautiful book, Robert Benson provides the sky in which your soul can soar. You *can* fly."

—**Leonard Sweet,** author of *The Gospel According to Starbucks*

"A rare treasure of a book. Robert Benson invites us into a heartfelt and humble journey of discovery of our calling via brokenness. Benson's generous language fills the reader's heart with godly wisdom, humor, and care. A must-read for all those struggling with the gap between deeper longings and the day-to-day struggles of our lives."

—**Makoto Fujimura,** founder of the International Arts Movement and author of *Images of Grace* and *Refractions: A Journey of Faith, Art, and Culture*

"The Robert Benson whom so many of us trust and enjoy has never been more open or wiser or funnier about vocation than he is here. Alternately candid and droll, lyrical and entertaining, he lays out the fruits of a lifetime and invites us to feast at will upon them. You will love this book."

—**Phyllis Tickle,** author of *The Words of Jesus: A Gospel of the Sayings of Our Lord* and *The Divine Hours*

"Benson makes a convincing argument that the voice we hear urging us to do the work we love could actually be the voice of the greatest lover of all. By the book's end, readers will smile to think that the vocational boxes we would like to check on our life résumé are the same boxes God has already selected for us."

—**Nancy Hull**, book reviewer for *Horn Book Review* and *The Grand Rapids Press* and author of *On Rough Seas*

"An insightful and sensitive book about the all-important subject of vocation."

—**Marcy Heidish**, author of *Soul and the City* and *A Woman Called Moses*

More Praise for Previous Books by Robert Benson

"Benson's tone remains chatty and down-to-earth, and the analogies he draws hit the mark."

—*The New York Times* **Book Review**

"Benson writes mellifluously with original insights and welcome humor.... [He] captures a world in which time slows down and material things become of less importance…. Charming and elegantly written…that rare gift, a thought-provoking record of his own spiritual quest… Willa Cather's phrase 'Thy will be done in art as it is in heaven' could serve as an epigraph to [his] fine work."

—*Publisher's Weekly*

"In looking at his own life with candor and hope, Robert Benson helps us to look at our own. His words have the ring of truth."

—**Frederick Buechner,** acclaimed author of more than thirty novels and nonfiction books, including *Secrets in the Dark* and *The Yellow Leaves*

"Robert Benson reminds us of what we too often forget— that the ground we walk upon is sacred. With the creative eye of a novelist and the playfulness of a poet, he tutors us in the art of really knowing the place where we live and celebrating the wonders in our own backyards."

—**Frederic and Mary Ann Brussat,** coauthors of *Spiritual Literacy* and directors of Spiritualityand Practice.com

FINDING YOUR TRUE CALLING

THE
ECHO
WITHIN

ROBERT BENSON

WATERBROOK
PRESS

THE ECHO WITHIN
PUBLISHED BY WATERBROOK PRESS
12265 Oracle Boulevard, Suite 200
Colorado Springs, Colorado 80921

Scriptures in this book are the author's paraphrases of the King James Version and the New English Bible. Copyright © 1961, 1970 by the Delegates of the Oxford University Press and the Syndics of the Cambridge University Press.

Details in some anecdotes and stories have been changed to protect the identities of the persons involved.

ISBN 978-0-3077-3046-6

Published in the United States by WaterBrook Multnomah, an imprint of the Crown Publishing Group, a division of Random House Inc., New York.

WATERBROOK and its deer colophon are registered trademarks of Random House Inc.

Library of Congress Cataloging-in-Publication Data
Benson, R. (Robert), 1952-
    The echo within : finding your true calling / Robert Benson.
— 1st ed.
        p. cm.
    Includes bibliographical references.
    ISBN 978-0-3077-3046-6
    1. Vocation—Religious aspects—Christianity. I. Title.
    BV4740.B47 2009
    248.4—dc22
                                                    2008034583

Printed in the United States of America
2011

10 9 8 7 6 5 4 3 2 1

SPECIAL SALES
Most WaterBrook Multnomah books are available in special quantity discounts when purchased in bulk by corporations, organizations, and special-interest groups. Custom imprinting or excerpting can also be done to fit special needs. For information, please e-mail SpecialMarkets@WaterBrookMultnomah.com or call 1-800-603-7051.

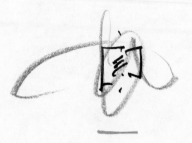

This book is for my father—
after all.

And, as always, it is for
the Friends of Silence and of the Poor,
whoever and wherever you may be.

—

And it is for Susan.

Namaste!

R.B.

Contents

Teach us in all things to seek first
Your honor and glory.
Grant that we may perceive the ways
in which You are calling to us,
and grant us strength and courage
to pursue those things
and to accomplish them.

—A COLLECT FOR GUIDANCE

one

Listening

My life is a listening, His is a speaking.

My salvation is to hear and respond.

—THOMAS MERTON

IT WAS EARLY FALL, and it was late afternoon, and I was walking through old Carolina pines with a new friend. We were near the ocean, near enough to hear the surf as we walked along a broad path through the forest.

I say I was with a new friend. I only spent five days with him, and I had never seen him before and have not seen him since. He and I were two of about sixty people at a retreat, and I was the speaker.

"I think I am being called to go to seminary," my new friend said. "Do you think I am?"

He was wrestling with a question that almost always arises whenever questions of calling are being raised. He was hoping I could tell him if he was being called by God to do a particular thing or if he was wanting to do it for his own reasons and giving God the credit. (Or the blame, perhaps?) He wanted me to look into the future and tell him which choice would be the right one. He was hoping I was a lot more than a speaker; he was hoping I was a prophet.

For a while I did the wisest thing I know to do in such a situation, which is to keep my mouth shut and listen.

We walked for a bit longer, and he talked a little more, and I tried to pay careful attention to the story he was telling me. We stopped for a moment to watch the sea and to listen to the surf.

"Sometimes," he said, "I cannot tell if it is God telling me this or if I am just talking to myself."

We watched the sea for a while.

"Exactly what does God's voice sound like?" I

asked him. "And how do you recognize that voice when you hear it?"

My new friend looked at me as though perhaps he should not be wasting his time with a guy who suddenly did not appear to be so prophetic after all.

I had clever follow-up questions too. "Does God sound like James Earl Jones or Helen Mirren? What if God sounds like Judi Dench or George Burns? What if God's voice is shrill and hard to listen to? What if God sounds like Truman Capote? What if the voice sounds like your own voice?"

These were not unreasonable questions to me on that day and are still not on this day. My new friend looked at me as though I had gone from being not as smart as he had hoped to being a smart aleck instead.

But I had a reason for asking those questions.

———

People go away on spiritual retreat for all kinds of reasons. I am one of those people. I think it is a good idea to go away for a while to listen for, and maybe even to, God.

It was my father who taught me to love going on retreat. He led so many of them that his father once asked him if he should not go on an advance for a change.

I think a retreat can be especially helpful when you are wrestling with some particular thing in your life. Having a leader or a teacher or a speaker there is a nice bonus, but it is not always the point. As the years go by, I go to fewer and fewer retreats where there is a speaker. Sometimes it is easier to listen for the voice of God if there is not someone else talking all the time.

I do not think I am necessarily right to think this way, but there it is. And I am glad everyone does not think this way, because I do like to go and be the speaker.

———

Some years ago I went away to become a member of the Academy for Spiritual Formation.

In simple terms the Academy is a program you attend once a quarter for two years, spending a week each time with the same sixty or so people—a week devoted to study, prayer, silence, worship, and community. The Academy is one part retreat, one part seminar, one part camp meeting, and one part small group.

That is why I have often said that in order to get the most out of the Academy, a person should be one part monk, one part dogface recruit, one part student, and seven parts hungry to learn to pray. There are not many things in this world that turn out to be more than the sum of the parts; the Academy is one of them.

The first week I listened carefully to everything as I was supposed to. Who I listened to most was a theologian and scholar named Robert Mulholland. And I have never gotten over one thing I remember from a whole week of listening to his lectures.

Dr. Mulholland is the one who introduced me to the Hebrew word *dabhar,* a word meaning "God spoke." *Dabhar* is the word used in Genesis, in the opening line of the beginning of the whole Story of us all. The word is most often rendered as *created* in our English translations.

"In the beginning God created the heavens and the earth" is the way the Story has always begun for many of us. And when you say it that way, creating the heavens and the earth sounds like the sort of thing one would do with his hands in the midst of the mother of all sandboxes.

I can imagine God down on holy knees somewhere in central Oklahoma scooping out the Mississippi until it gets to the Gulf of Mexico. Then God takes a handful or two of the extra dirt and pushes forward and to the right, and soon we have the Appalachians running all the way up to where Canada will be, once we need a place called Canada. The earth gives way under the left knee, and God decides the Rockies have a kind of majestic look to them after all of that flat land that is going to be Kansas. Kansas is going to be beautiful when all the grasses have been planted there and they have time to learn to go golden in the sun. Somebody will write songs about these flatlands someday, about amber waves of grain and purple mountains, once somebodies have been made, and once they have had time to learn to write songs.

Then there are oceans to be made and more mountains on the other side of the earth. There are stars to be hung in the night sky, "God's sweet lanterns," as James Taylor once described them. And on and on. Thinking about the creation of the universe in this way makes me smile.

Here is another thing that makes me smile: after all of this time, we do not really understand the ways of God, do we? Not even after all of these years of telling each other this Story and having people try and explain the Story to us. All of our theology and scholarship and imagination notwithstanding, we do not even have a good handle on the way the whole thing started.

Saint Augustine once said to a group of people, "We are talking about God. What wonder is it that you do not understand? If you do understand, it is not God."

We keep trying though. We keep trying to understand the mysterious ways of God. Which is why the word *dabhar* caught my attention and has never quite let it go. I am still trying to hold the wonder of the word and how the word itself has changed the way I have come to see the way we were made.

According to the people who told this Story first, in the Hebrew language and not the king's English, the making of the heavens and the earth, and all that came to be, for that matter, was for God a thing done with the voice rather than the hands. *Dabhar* suggests an understanding of the way God creates that is very different from my vision of God in a sandbox.

Dabhar means we are more accurate if we say, "In the beginning God spoke the heavens and the earth." *Dabhar* means God spoke the mountains and the seas. God spoke the mornings and the trees and the streams and the songbirds. God spoke the stars, those sweet lanterns, and God spoke the plains and the amber waves of grain. God spoke the roses that climb up on the roof of my studio, and God spoke the breeze that tells me the rain is soon to come, the rain God spoke into being this morning when God said let there be light all over again.

In those days when I was listening to Bob Mulholland, I was also learning to pray the Psalms. I have not gotten over what the Psalmists said any more than I have gotten over what Bob Mulholland said.

In the ninety-fifth one, the Psalmist writes, "We will know your power and presence this day, if we will but listen for your voice." I had always taken the phrase to mean we are to listen for the voice of the God without. And it is true. We are to listen for the way God speaks to us through the breeze and through the rain, through the voice of a friend and the laughter of a child, through the thousand other ways God speaks into our lives.

But we are to learn to listen for and to recognize the voice of God within us as well.

We are, said Bob Mulholland, "an incarnate word, spoken by God, still being spoken by God." And because we are still being spoken, the questions we have about calling are, in part, questions about listening for the incarnate word being whispered into us. They are questions about learning to open up to and becoming the word that was whispered into us. And is still being whispered into us.

I was listening carefully to Psalm 139 in those days too: "We thank You that we are so marvelously made and that we were not hidden from You when we were being made in secret in the depths of the earth. You knew us before we even were."

With apologies to the Psalmist, I was not simply fearfully and wonderfully and marvelously made. I was fearfully and wonderfully and marvelously spoken into being. And so were you.

Somewhere deep inside of me, perhaps in the truest and most holy part of me—the part of me that is the most me there is or ever will be—there is an echo of the Voice that spoke me into being and is still speaking the incarnate word who is Robert.

If I can learn to recognize that Voice, I may also learn to trust it.

———

There is within me a small voice I know to pay attention to.

It is the voice that tells me I have to change the way I am doing this thing or that one, the voice that tells me to go slowly about this or about that.

It is the voice that says to me this person or that one is going to be important in my life, the voice that says to me the time has come to move in another direction.

It is the voice I depend on to warn me and rebuke me, to cheer me on and to wake me up, to settle me down and to lift me up.

I know and trust and count on that voice for many things. I also know that voice sounds a lot like me.

———

"To listen to you or to listen to Me," said Jesus to those who would follow Him, "is not to hear you or Me; it is to hear the One Who sent Me."

I am coming to believe that the small voice within me is an echo of the Voice that is still speaking the incarnate word that I am here to become, an echo of the Voice that spoke us all into being, an echo of the Voice that spoke all that is alive.

Sometimes we are hesitant to trust that small voice within us because we think it is just ourselves doing the talking and could not possibly be an echo of the Voice of the One Who made us. Sometimes we do not trust that voice within us simply because it sounds like our own voice. Sometimes we are afraid to trust that voice because we have heard a similar voice inside us say things that are hurtful and angry and hateful, to ourselves and about others.

We must learn to listen deeper and deeper, seeking out the true voice within us that echoes the Voice of the One Who made us.

Thomas Merton, the Trappist monk, knew this to be true: "For if I find Him, I will find myself, and if I find myself, I will find Him."

"I must find him in what I am or not at all," writes H. A. Williams.

We worry that we are just talking to ourselves. If it sounds like me, it cannot be God, we think. And so we are afraid to trust what we hear, afraid to trust that voice that has been within us all along.

The fact that the Voice that calls to us often sounds like our own is not something to be mistrusted or feared. It is a sign of how close God is to us.

We can trust that Voice when it is calling to us, and we can trust that Voice when it speaks for us.

———

In Carolina that afternoon, my new friend and I worked our way back through the forest to the spot near the lodge where we had begun. Our walk was over. As often happens, we had worked our way back to the original question as well.

We stood for a moment in the breeze, looking for a way to gather up the loose ends and declare the conversation done. He said again, "I am not sure if God is telling me this or if it is only me talking."

"Perhaps there is no difference," I said to him. "Perhaps you should listen to that voice within that sounds so much like your own. Just because it sounds like you does not mean you cannot trust it."

There is within each of us an echo of the Voice of the One Who whispered us into being. We must listen for that echo and to that echo; we must listen fiercely and faithfully and fearlessly. Within the echo of the Voice that spoke us into being is the sound of our own true voice.

two

Waking

The spiritual life is, then, first of all
a matter of keeping awake.

—THOMAS MERTON

IT IS A FEW DAYS BEFORE CHRISTMAS. Mr. Kennedy is in the White House, Mr. Mantle patrols the outfield for the Yankees, Mr. King has yet to march, and Mr. McCartney and Mr. Lennon are working in small clubs in Liverpool.

Computers are only for the scientists, a three-point play in basketball requires one to hit a foul shot, all three television channels are in black and white at my house, and some men still wear fedoras and often wear ties when they go out in public. Especially if they are going to the office, which is where I am going and why I have on my tie.

I am ten years old, and I am walking as quickly as I can so I can keep up with my father as he heads north up the sidewalk along Fourth Avenue in Nashville.

He is taking me with him to the office on this particular day because I am out of school for the holiday and need something to do and because his office Christmas party is today. Years later, when I had children of my own and took them to the office to show them off to my friends, I wondered whether the father or the son most enjoyed that long-ago holiday visit to my father's office.

I am excited to be going. At ten years old, I do not get to be a grownup often, though I want to be one terribly, even then. I have on my Sunday clothes.

We walk toward a row of old brick buildings, two or three stories tall. On the left is the parking lot behind the original Ryman Auditorium, the first home of the Grand Ole Opry. The row of buildings that made up the Benson printing plant to which my father and I were headed that December day is gone now. To this day I wonder why people who are going to renew the urban always begin with a wrecking ball. Such a thing is not renewal; it is replacement. A fair amount of everything two generations of my Benson forebears worked to build disappeared one week somewhere between the 1964 World's Fair and the 1968 Democratic Convention in Chicago.

We could not foresee much of what was to come, not on that December morning—not the wrecking ball or the rock'n'roll, not Dallas or Selma, not Memphis or Los Angeles, not Tet or Watts, not any of the things that would shape us all before the end of the sixties. And they were the things that shaped all of us, even those among us who do not recognize the names or remember what happened in those places.

Walking with my father toward the old Benson building, I am headed to the place where one day I will begin to hear my calling. As much as anywhere, this is the place where I took my first steps in the direction of responding to that calling, my first steps toward trying to become the person I was spoken into being to become. All of the roads I have traveled since began in that place.

I am headed that day toward Eden in a way, if Eden can be the name for a place where all things begin, a place where our journey starts. This is certainly the place where my journey in the direction of my calling began.

Our Edens are not the same. And I do not know what yours was like, that place where your journey began. But I do know there were things in the place you began—sights and sounds and smells and rituals and work—that have played some part in your sense of your calling and in the work you do each day. Some of them drew you toward something; some of them may have pushed you away.

Eden has always smelled like paper and ink to me.

I can put my nose in a book and close my eyes and draw in a deep breath, and a whole world comes back to me. It is a world of printing presses and bindery machines, of dust and paper, of skids piled high with boxes of books, a world of forklifts hauling to and fro, of tape machines and page trimmers, of oily rags and engraving acid. I went through those doors once when I was young and entered the world of books, a world that has been drawing me ever since.

My first memories of the old printing plant are from the times I would visit with my dad. We would work our way through the corridors, and my father would say hello to people he knew—my grandfather and the uncles and cousins, friends and associates. I can recall only a few of the faces, and I suspect many of them only remembered me as Bob's boy, if they remembered me at all.

I come from a long line of folks who had ink in their blood. Or if not in their blood, then the ink was at least on their hands—writers and editors and publishers and printing salesmen.

Not surprisingly, I fell in love with the paper and ink, the tools it took to lay out the pages, the rhythm of the presses, the book boxes, and the shipping-room dust. The physicality of the book itself and of the making of it was powerful and precious to me. I loved books long before I started writing them.

My great-grandfather started the printing company and the music publishing company that were in these buildings. He was gone well before I came along; I never knew him.

My father worked in the music company. I did too when I was young.

My first job was in that building. I was twelve.

My grandfather hired my cousin and me to cut a page out of a hymn book, a page that mistakenly had a song that the denomination for whom he had printed the hymnal did not want to sing.

We spent our summer cutting out the offending page with a knife. Someone down in the bindery, a professional we supposed, was going to glue in a new page, tipping it in along the small stub left where we made our cut. I have a scar on my thumb from those days, from a slip of the knife.

All through high school and then into college, I worked summers and weekends there. I spent a lot of hot, dusty days down in the belly of those old buildings, hauling boxes and unloading trucks mostly. I finally was promoted to the mailroom and got to be in one of the air-conditioned parts of the place.

I was happy to be cooler, but I missed the smell of the ink and the rhythmic clatter of the presses. I still do.

Annie Dillard tells of asking a painter what made him decide to become a painter. "I liked the smell of the paint," he told her.

I know a farmer in Mississippi who will get tears in his eyes talking about the rich earth in the Delta and a lump in his throat at the sight of the first green shoots of corn in the spring. I know a chef who likes his work because he gets to play with knives and fire all day. (I am glad he is in a kitchen.) A woman in our neighborhood missed the exotic flavors of the popsicles she ate when she was a little girl in Mexico. Last week's flavor of the week in her popsicle store had jalapeños and chocolate, something I never got from the popsicle man when I was a boy.

We can be awakened to our calling, drawn in the direction of it, in different ways. For some of us it is the smell of the paint, the feel of a page, the warmth of a stove, the sound of a tool. Others of us awakened in other ways—a conversation with a teacher, an article we read and could not forget, a photograph that showed us a place we thought we could belong to someday.

Some thing catches our attention and rings true within us. It resonates with the echo within us, one might say, and we are off, off on the journey to discover what we have been spoken into being to become.

I started out being drawn by ink on paper and eventually came to be drawn to the people who wrote the words. By the time I was in high school, I was absolutely in love with word people—people who wrote them or edited them, quoted them or sang them, honored them and loved them. They were people who had great collections of words on the shelves in their houses. They were people who thought a life lived working among words was a life worth living.

All of which is to say that in my case the apple did not fall far from the tree.

My apple, the whole tree for that matter, came with ink stains. I took it as a sign.

———

At a writer's conference once, in a question-and-answer session, a woman asked the speaker what steps she should take in order to become a writer. She also asked if the speaker thought she could actually achieve that goal.

The speaker was me. And I told her I would try to answer the questions as best I could.

I first suggested that she arrange to be born into a publishing family so she could grow up around printers and writers and poets and musicians and artists.

I also told her I had discovered that writing bad poetry during high school, lots of it, seems to be critical. Dropping out of college a few times, having gone only to the English lit classes with any regularity, makes a contribution that is unclear but necessary, at least in my experience.

It helped me, I think, to work in business for a while until I finally caught on that I was not cut out for business after all. I recommend moving off to a big city where you know only one person but you talk that person into paying you by the hour to write advertising copy so you can learn to make sentences people will read, just in case you ever get to write on your own someday.

Then move back home and open your own agency. Go through a divorce; lose almost everything; land a job with a set of fine publishing folks who will take you in when you are desperate for work. Be a bad employee so the same set of fine folks will fire you after two years. Be grateful they took you in, and be grateful they let you go.

Because then you get to write your first book and discover at last that writing books is the only thing you want to do, maybe even the only thing you know how to do, and certainly the only thing that sensible people will allow you to do.

With my tongue firmly planted in my cheek, I concluded, "This particular method has produced a writer every time it has been tried. It is a foolproof process. And this fool," I said, pointing at myself, "guarantees it will work for you, if you do the steps just the way I did them."

The woman at the conference looked at me as though I were crazy. And she was closer to being right about that than she knew. I had left out the part about being in the psych ward for a while between the bankruptcy and the being fired. A psych ward is not for everyone, but if the right circumstances land on you, then do not pass on any invitation that comes your way. My stay in the psych ward is one of the three best things that ever happened to me.

I should have told her that I am still a little crazy, and I have the papers to prove it.

All of our journeys are different, whether we are moving toward becoming a writer or a teacher or a soldier or a nurse or a carpenter. In some way that I am not sure I can explain, looking at our journeys intently, following the arc of the stories they tell us, helps us to listen for the parts of those journeys that resonate with the echo within.

"Listen to your life. See it for the fathomless mystery that it is," writes Frederick Buechner. "In the boredom and pain of it no less than in the excitement and gladness: touch, taste, smell your way to the holy and hidden heart of it."

I am not wise enough to know exactly what the woman at the conference must learn to listen for in the story of her life. And I do not know whether or not what she hears there will lead her to the writing life. I will never be able to hear the word that was whispered into her.

The truth is that it takes all of the courage and all of the love and all of the hope I can muster just to hear what my own life is saying to me. It takes all of my attention to hear the echo of the word that was whispered into me. I cannot listen for anyone else.

———

I was thirteen when I first began to hear what I was being called to be. But I did not tell anyone for a long time.

Emmet Fox writes of "the most secret, sacred wish that lies deep down at the bottom of your heart, the wonderful thing that you hardly dare to look at, or to think about…because it seems so far beyond anything that you are." To say such a wonder aloud was too much for me when I was young.

For a while I kept to the original and official dream of all the little boys I knew, though my chances of becoming the second baseman for the Yankees were never very high. One curve ball from Markie Webb, high and inside, on a Little League afternoon took care of that. He did not hit me in the head, but once I realized such a thing was a possibility, my dream of working in the House That Ruth Built began to fade.

Then I was going to be a rock star. We all were going to be rock stars; it was the early sixties. A distinct lack of musical talent proved to be a major obstacle to my musical career.

Then I worked very hard to become a publisher like my father and his father. Having no head for business took care of that, though several years of labor were required before that fact made itself known to me. Or before I would admit it is perhaps a more accurate way to say it.

For almost a decade, I was certain I was going to become a fabulous and wealthy creative director in a renowned advertising agency, but that did not work out so well either. I did not like the work for one thing.

Then I became an editor for a small publishing house. For a few weeks I was very happy there. Until I found out that the people who hired me thought I should come to the office every day and behave myself in meetings and read and write long reports.

Every time I made a move, I thought I was being called to be something different, to head in another direction, to pursue another dream. In some ways I was right every time. Even though for a long time, most of my adult life, it looked as though I was avoiding my true calling altogether.

One day I was sitting through a meeting at the publishing company where I had the last job I ever had. A great discussion ensued about whether or not God has a particular plan for each of our lives. It is a discussion one runs into around church folks.

At the time one or two of the dozen or so folks in the room seemed absolutely certain God was directing every last detail of our individual lives. They suggested that everything was so mapped out that one could get into a fair amount of trouble with the Creator of the universe by not filling in all of one's blanks correctly. There was also talk about wasting gifts and burying talents and fields ripe for the harvest. Saint Paul was quoted a good deal, which always makes for a lively discussion. We church folks spend a lot of time arguing over some of the things Saint Paul wrote in his letters to his friends in the ancient church. As is often the case when Christians talk about Saint Paul, it did not take long for our discussion to go from lively to heated.

One of my friends in the room, a quiet man, held his counsel for a long while. He could not hold out forever though; we often looked to him for the last word.

Finally he was pressed into the corner.

Yes, he said, he did believe God had a particular plan for each of us. Furthermore, he said, he even knew what it was for each of us. Which was considerably further than I expected him to go.

"The plan is for you to become the person God intended. However," he said with a generous twinkle in his eye, "the details are up to you."

"This is the time to strain," writes Mark Van Doren, "to pull at yourself until you assume the shape which is to be yours uniquely and permanently."

Your Eden is your Eden; it is your starting point and only yours. Any resemblance to someone else's starting point is purely coincidental. You wander through your Eden; you listen as fiercely as you can; you watch yourself closely to see what you love and what you do not. You look for signs of your own wonder. You look for the things that make your spirit quicken and your pulse race.

You look for the thing that appears to be light in the midst of your dark. You venture forth; you answer the bell; you take the call; you try something new on for size. You claim you are being called to do so. And you are right, every time.

Where it all takes you is where you have been meant to go all along. The details have been up to you all along as well.

———

On that long-ago late December morning, I knew none of these things.

I was just happy to be going to the office with my father, happy a journey was upon us, even though I had no idea where it would lead. But something began to ring true to me that day; something began to resonate with the echo within.

three

Hearing

The spiritual life is first of all a *life*.
It is not merely something to be known
and studied, it is to be lived.

—Thomas Merton

I AM WORKING MY WAY through a crowd of folks in a hallway of a convention center. I am a young man, in my thirties, and five or six of the men I admire most, men whose approval I want more than anyone else's in the world, are standing in a circle talking.

I feel as if I have known them all of my life, and almost have. They are my father's closest publishing friends, his best friends for some twenty years. I have not seen them all together like this in a long time, not since my father passed away, and I head in their direction.

One of them sees me coming, and he grins. "Here he is," Mac says with his customary enthusiasm—the enthusiasm for which he is best known, enthusiasm with enough power to have made a fair number of us believe we might be able to become more than we ever dreamed we could be. Even now you can stand in certain convention halls, with thousands of music people around, and close your eyes and throw a dodge ball and hit someone for whom Mac's enthusiasm and encouragement changed the course of his life.

He puts his arm around me and presents me to the circle as though they have never seen me before in their lives. "Here he is. If there is ever going to be a real writer among us, this is he."

At the time I believe this is as good a thing as anyone has ever said to me. Later I remember I should do what everyone else did when Mac said such things— divide by three. No one was ever as good or as bad as Mac would declare them to be.

When I remember the moment now, I imagine a baton being passed.

———

There is a line I can trace through my life connecting a list of folks who said a particular thing to me at a particular moment, and what they said and the fact that I heard them and acted upon what I heard has made all of the difference. Some of what they said affected the way I spend my hours and days and the work I do. But there is more to the list than that.

Your vocation is not only about the work you do with your hands and your heart and your mind; it is about what shapes the work, about the person you become in and around that work as well. Vocation is also about the things that shape the work before the worker even begins to work.

Calling is not always static; it is not always a one-time event. And the Voice that calls us can also be heard without us as well as within us.

———

In my memory I can see the schoolroom where one of my teachers first told me she thought I had a way with words.

I can also see the campfire at the end of a church retreat one fall, the one where I made a promise or two—promises I discovered years later I had found a way to keep.

If I go a few blocks from my house, I pass the corner where I stood next to a church and met Russell for the first time. Not too far away is the neighborhood where I spent all those days at Mac's house when I was a boy.

The place where I used to meet Ben and the place where I first met Danny are within three miles of my house and within a hundred yards of each other. If you keep connecting the dots in the story of my life, you go from there to Sumatanga and Cincinnati, to Memphis and San Antonio, none of them places I ever lived but places I was in when a word was said to me at the precise moment I needed to hear one.

The line goes from Alice to Bob to Russell to Mac to Ben to Danny to W. to Ed to Phyllis to Fred. Most of them do not know any of the others, have never even met them. And there were more in between and more since, too many to name and kind souls all, who encouraged and pushed and shaped and nudged me along.

I am not the only one with such a list.

When we stop and listen our way through the stories of our lives, those characters are there once again. They are the grownups in our lives in the days we were growing up. They are the teachers and coaches who taught us and shaped us. They are neighbors, and they are mentors, and they are wise uncles and aunts.

They are people with whom we worked and whose influence still is found on our lives. They are old colleagues and associates; they are fellow pilgrims and seekers; they are lifelong friends and companions.

I remember what each of them said to me, the sentences themselves, the words that meant so much to me and to my sense of who I was and who I might become. I even have all of the sentences scribbled down in a book, though unnecessarily so: all of the words are written on my heart.

The people who said them never remember they said them. Whenever I have tried to thank them, they have invariably replied, "I said that?"

Most of the sentences are ordinary. And not one of them was said to me while I was talking to these people about vocation or calling. In some cases the meeting itself was an accident. In others it was one brief encounter, a few moments in a lifetime of talking and hearing, a few moments that changed the life I have lived from that moment on.

—

You know you have heard such a sentence when you hear inside a corresponding *yes*. The yes is an echo of sorts, an echo that you have come to count on.

Such a sentence takes your breath away when you first hear it, and then again when you repeat it to yourself later. The words tell you something about yourself you suspected or hoped, something you glimpsed but were too shy or uncertain to name aloud.

The sentence becomes a sort of touchstone for you as you wander and wonder your way along in search of your calling, in search of your work, in search of what comes next. One sentence builds on the previous ones, and some new thing begins to form in your heart or in your mind, sometimes right in front of you—a new opportunity, a new way of working, a new crowd of folks to work beside, a new way of understanding your place in the world.

———

You have to be careful when it comes to these things. Temptation is everywhere.

One temptation is to take almost every sentence and turn it into a commentary on your life and your calling. Not every sermon you hear, every article you read, every deep conversation with a wise one or a friend has to be about your calling or will be. I am not certain who first said that a watched pot never boils. But she would have had something to say about constantly keeping one's ear tuned in for life-changing sentences. Most often you cannot find this stuff; it comes to find you when you least expect it.

We are often tempted to try too hard, to be in too big a hurry, to try to make something out of nothing. If we are not careful, we can be blown about by every conversation we have with anyone who matters to us.

And we can be going too fast to hear clearly. Hearing clearly often requires waiting patiently.

Another temptation is to wait for God to write all of the answers on our wall one night while we are asleep. Which often keeps us from listening to things being said by the people God uses to say such things. Which is what really happens most of the time.

As often as not, someone else does the talking when God has some new thing for us to hear. It is one of God's better tricks, if you ask me. This is true whether people are aware of it or not or are willing to admit it or not. Sometimes people hesitate to give God any credit for being able to work through the ordinary of our lives, through the very sentences we hear and say.

Such touchstone sentences are affirmations, not commands; they illumine rather than instruct. They help you get your bearings, but they do not offer marching orders. They will nudge you a point or two toward starboard or port but rarely turn you 180 degrees.

They do not say where you are going next as much as they reinforce the direction in which you are heading. To the degree they point you toward a new road, it will most always be a new road with which you are already familiar.

"Be not afraid," said the One Who came. You may as well take Him at His word.

Be not afraid to wander and wonder along. Do not fear trying to find your way and, from time to time, being lost along that same way. If you will be patient—and patience is not a virtue in these matters but a necessity—a sentence or two will be given to you.

You will know it has happened when the echo within you says yes in return, in response to some sentence offered up that seems to resonate with what you are hearing in the echo within.

You will know at least this: for the moment, you are on the right road.

four

Being

Yet before we can surrender ourselves

we must become ourselves.

For no one can give up what he does not possess.

—THOMAS MERTON

A FRIEND OF MINE told me about a Sunday night when she was a teenager, a Sunday night when a missionary came and conducted the evening service at the church she and her family attended. I know what these services were like because missionaries came and did the same sort of Sunday evening services at our church as well. There was the obligatory slide show of native culture and people sitting in circles under banyan trees with Bibles in their laps, if the Bible had indeed been translated into their language. There were pictures of vast outback landscapes that could only be negotiated by something sturdier than the car we rode in to get to church.

Such missionary presentations were one of the chief ways to raise money for mission work. The services were also a primary way to recruit people into the work itself.

There was generally a good deal of squirming in the teenager section during these presentations. We were often nervous that we might be called to the mission field. What most of us wanted to do was to finish high school and live a normal sort of life. "Here am I, Lord; send me" made for great discussion in a Sunday school class, but none of us wanted to go anywhere that required we do anything too hard. That is the way I remember it. My friend tells the story from another perspective, albeit a short-lived one.

She says that on one of those evenings, she was not squirming at all. In fact, she began to seriously consider going to the mission field. She was not sure exactly what was drawing her, but she suspected that this was the moment to offer herself up to some larger thing. She went home from church and told her father she was hoping to be called to the mission field. Her father looked at her for a long minute, and then he grinned. He knew his daughter well.

"Honey," he said, "you just want to drive one of those Jeeps."

———

Ritually in our society, toward the end of a person's second decade on the planet, and even earlier sometimes, a small army of well-intentioned grownups starts to ask questions of the young people under their care and tutelage and influence.

"What are you going to do when you grow up?" is the question they ask, over and over, in one of its various and sundry guises. There are dozens of subtle and not-so-subtle ways to ask the question.

There is the guidance counselor version of the question. "Are you preparing to enter college or preparing to enter the world of work?" Of course, guidance counselors rarely mention that college graduates do not immediately go on to live a life of leisure but end up having to work themselves.

There is the parental approach. "Do you understand that even though we have enjoyed cleaning up after you for years, you cannot stay here forever?" This is the question perceptive parents ask when they begin to see that the nest is actually supposed to be empty someday.

And there is the youth pastor inquiry. "What do you think God is calling you to do?" This is often the point at which we are taught to separate the world of work into two worlds—the holy and the profane, the sacred and the secular, as though only a chosen few are called to do the work of building the kingdom and the rest of us are to spend our work lives hanging on for dear life.

Right in there somewhere, between the ages of sixteen and twenty-two, we are asked all these questions and more. The questions ask us to make a choice or two or twenty-seven that will go a long way toward determining the kind of work we do and the way we do the work and what the work will mean to us and for us for the rest of our lives. The questions come fast and furious, and the consequences of not answering quickly and correctly seem huge. So we answer as best we can.

At the time we try to fire back the answers, most of us are only guessing. And not all of us, maybe not many of us, are right the first time.

I am not surprised that so few people manage to stumble into their true vocation right out of the box, so to speak, given such a way of doing things. The surprise is that anyone ever manages to do that at all. Some folks are better guessers than others, I suppose.

It is what happens to the rest of us in that moment—with our whole future in front of us, with someone who matters to us awaiting our answer—that interests me.

———

How in the world do we make choices about what we are going to do all our lives when we are not yet old enough to know who we are?

"The Ancients said, 'Know thyself,' and the moderns say, 'Be yourself,'" write E. Graham Howe and

L. Le Mesurier. "It is not the same thing, but the recommendations do not conflict, and may even be necessary to each other's fulfillment."

They go on.

"But what is this 'self,' and how are we to know it?"

———

When I was in high school, I quickly learned I was "other" in a lot of ways. I was quieter and more serious than most. Except for the fact that I could not use a slide rule, I would have been a nerd. I was different enough to be uncomfortable most of the time. I was almost forty before I began to learn the reasons why I was so other. The unpacking of my otherness began at the Academy for Spiritual Formation.

By the third day of my first week at the Academy, even though we were all still reading name badges so we could call each other by name, I was comfortable among the whole crowd of people. I felt as though I had always belonged there, as though I had always known and been known by these folks. I rarely felt that way in my own family, much less in a crowd of strangers.

I did not understand this sudden sense of belonging at all, but then there were a lot of things I did not understand during the first week at the Academy.

I did not understand why we took a personality test during the first week. A personality test seemed an odd thing for a prayer community to do.

I was resistant to taking the test in the first place. I was mostly afraid the results would show I had little or no personality whatsoever. Or that the one I had would be pronounced unlikable. Or remedial work might be involved.

In the second week, we were given our test results by the expert who had given us the test. (To this day I wonder about the qualifications for being a personality expert. Are you required to already have a winning personality, or can you get one in graduate school?) She helped us begin to discover things about ourselves—the way we take in and process information, the way we face the world and its problems and its questions, the way we interact with people, the way we make decisions. She did not make value judgments about my personality or the lack thereof as I feared she might.

I discovered, among other things, that out of every hundred people gathered up in a room somewhere, there would rarely be anyone else in the room with my personality profile. In a room with three hundred people, there might be as many as two others; if I could find those two, we might be friends. Our finding each other is not likely, as shy as the three of us are likely to be, according to the personality profile.

The other thing I discovered was that of the sixty-five or so of us there in the Academy, more than fifty of us had roughly the same sort of profile.

I was in the only room I had ever been in, in my whole life, in which I was not automatically other.

———

This late-in-life glimpse into the workings of my mind and heart let me see into the way I am, the way I *be*, if you will.

The more I learned about my own sweet self—the self I wanted to offer to God in service to the work of God in the world—the more I learned why many of the things I had tried to do had not worked so well.

Given the nature of the way I was fearfully and wonderfully whispered into being, becoming a highly successful businessman was not ever much of a possibility. Nor was being a treasured member of the church board or a productive salesperson or an executive.

On the one hand, the information was exhilarating. For the first time in my life, I could see that the things that made me so other were not the result of character flaws or lack of willpower or defective social skills. They were simply a function of my being wired differently from other folks. They were a reflection of the difference between what makes up the incarnate word *Robert* that was whispered into me and what makes up the incarnate word *Rebecca* or *Richard* or *Robin* that has been whispered into someone else.

The test explained to me how and why I was drawn to certain things—including what has become my life's work, which I had long suspected was to be my life's work and into which I was about to finally wander.

On the other hand, the information made me sad to know that at the ripe old age of eighteen, all those years ago, I had gone out to go and *do* long before I had much idea of who I *be*.

I found myself wondering about the places I might have gone, the people I might have known, the things I might have written had I known more about who I was when I left home. I found myself thinking back on the twenty years between that day I packed some stuff into a VW and headed off to college and this day on which I was learning about who I be for the first time. I thought about work I had done poorly, people I had hurt, promises I had not been able to keep.

These days, every time I talk to young people who are just beginning their journey into the world of vocation and calling and work, I wonder if they know any more about who they be than I did when I set forth.

I want to ask them to keep a journal, to make a daily habit of writing down the things that move them, the things that bore them, the things that make them sing. I want them to learn how powerful it is to go back through your journals each year, reading your own story to see what your story is telling you now, to hear what it says to you of the echo within.

I want to tell them to take advantage of the tools that modern psychology has to offer, the personality tests and such, to not be afraid of or intimidated by such instruments. "There is only one thing you should do," wrote Rilke to a young man. "Go into yourself." Any tool that will help is a welcome one.

I want to tell them to trust the instincts that have been whispered into them, trust the sense of what makes them feel whole as it resonates with the incarnate word whispered into them, trust that the One Who made them has given them the ability to hear the echo within.

———

What might it mean to any one of us to have a better sense of the way we are made?

It could help us know whether we are more comfortable in solitude or in a crowd. It could help us know whether we make our decisions with our head or our heart.

It could help us know the sorts of work for which we are best suited before we choose the work we will pursue.

How many of us end up doing work that does not suit us, in environments that do not nurture us, around people with whom we are not comfortable, doing things we do not believe in?

When I started out, what might it have meant to have had some better sense of the tone and color and timbre and subtlety of the echo within me, the echo of the incarnate word within that is Robert?

What might such a thing mean to any of us? Whether we are starting out or starting over.

Even though there have been some bumps and bruises along the way, there is enough joy and wonder and love and grace in the life to which I am given these days that to complain about the road I have traveled would be ungrateful at the very least. And there is no question that some of what I learned while wandering through those places that did not suit me very well has turned out to be invaluable for the work I have now been given to do. I am perfectly happy to stand up and sing two choruses of the old gospel song we sang when I was growing up—"I Wouldn't Take Nothing for My Journey Now."

But I still wonder what might have happened had I known more about myself and how I was made when I was so young and required to make such choices.

Some things would have likely turned out the same. I cannot say for certain, but no one else can either.

I was always called to do the work I am now doing. I believe I knew it when I was young.

And all of those years of moving from place to place, masquerading as a businessman, wandering along in the desert looking for the trail to Canaan with Moses and the rest may or may not have been the only way for me to get here.

But I may have done myself a disservice when I tried to answer a question about what I might do without knowing much about who I be.

Knowing more about who we are might keep more of us from making the journey toward what we do harder than it has to be.

Knowing who we are might keep us from trying to be someone else. I might have sat through a lot fewer meetings wearing a necktie. I might have spent a lot less time trying to be a publisher when I should have been trying to learn to write a sentence. I might have spent a lot less time trying to act like a businessman when I really am a writer.

Knowing more about who we are is the sort of information that might keep us from heading off to the mission field when all we really want is to drive a Jeep.

five

Looking

Find God first in the community,

then He will lead you to solitude.

—THOMAS MERTON

I READ AN INTERVIEW with Doris Betts, one of the fine southern novelists of our time. She claimed she writes her books for a jury of twelve.

Some of the people in her jury box are people who are always there, for every book. Her family is always in the jury, for example. But the other members of the jury change depending on the book she is writing. When she sits down to write, she sees the faces of real people she knows, not a large unknown and faceless audience out there somewhere.

Frederick Buechner advises, "Write to someone you love and someone who knows you well. You use your real voice with those you love and you cannot be phony with those who know you well."

Somewhere between the two of them, I began to learn something about writing and about calling.

These days, before I begin to write a book, I take a fountain pen and a piece of good sketch paper and draw a set of twelve boxes. I think about for whom I am writing the book that I am about to begin. I write their names in the boxes. Then I take stickpins and put the diagram of my jury on the wall in front of the table where I write. That way while I am working, we can keep an eye on each other, so to speak.

For me, a book is a series of stories I tell to the jury, a series of stories that I think go together somehow. I tell the stories, and as I go along, I try to discover what they might mean to me as well as the jurors. It is not exactly one story per juror; nothing about writing a book is ever that neat and tidy for me.

The trick to this, the important thing to me, is to

keep looking my jury in the eye. Keep writing sentences to them and for them. They are the ones to whom I have been given and who have been given to me for this particular bit of my work.

———

I kept a low profile for the first couple of years I attended the cathedral where I am now a member. In the church I attended before I joined the cathedral, I unwittingly attempted to set a record for a layperson's involvement in the life and work of a local church.

I went to church on Sundays to worship and to lead the class I had started. I went on Mondays to check in with staff on promotional materials for upcoming events; in those days I wrote and produced them all. I went on Tuesdays for the committee or board meetings. I went on Wednesdays to take my children to choir practice and to take the Eucharist. I went on Thursdays for small-group meetings.

If you had asked me to, I could have easily made the case that I was simply honoring my God-given gifts and talents. I could do some of those things as well if not better than anyone else in the church. And I could have made a case for my being called to do all of them, simply because I could do them so well.

And it was all good work, work that needed to be done. Or I supposed it did. And the church folks were happy for me to volunteer for everything and anything; the more I could do, the better. Which led to my finally burning out altogether.

Which was more my fault than theirs, but it happened just the same.

A couple of years later I left that church for other reasons and ended up a member of the parish at the cathedral. And I was determined not to let the same thing happen.

My experience is that if church folks find out you can teach a class or lead a retreat or have an idea at a meeting, then they will give you a fair number of chances to do exactly that. So I kept my head down.

For a couple of years, I was tempted not to use my real name. I thought of it as being in the Layman's Protection Program.

Eventually I started feeling guilty about not ever doing anything around the church, so I decided to talk to the dean of the cathedral. I had lunch once a month with the dean. It was not exactly a ministry on my part; he always bought, for one thing.

One day we had lunch right around the time of the big parish fair, the annual event where the different ministries and groups in the parish try to get folks to sign up to participate.

I told him I felt guilty about never doing anything much around the church. He listened as I told him my burnout story. I said I thought perhaps I was ready to do more.

Then he told me the work I did outside the parish — writing books and leading retreats and speaking at conferences and all that makes up the work to which I have been called and to which I have been given — might well be the work I was to give to the parish, after all was said and done.

"There are more than two thousand of us in this parish, and we can find someone to take the kids on retreat and someone to coach the basketball team and someone to teach the Sunday school classes and someone to run the stewardship committee," he told me. "We cannot find someone to do what you do."

He looked me in the eye.

"Write your books, say your prayers, lead your retreats. And when you can, be here with us and bring whatever your work makes of you and park yourself in the pew next to the rest of us when we gather up to worship."

In a way, what he meant was for me to keep an eye on my jury box.

We church folks sometimes do things in the name of ministry and vocation for a host of other reasons. Just because it is done in and around a crowd of church folks does not mean it is a ministry. Just because we think God approves of what we are doing does not mean it is a calling.

Some questions we have about finding our calling and vocation are *what* questions. What God-given gifts do I have? What can I do? What is being asked of me?

And some of them are *where* questions. Where is the right place for me? Do I still want to work here? Is this school the right one for me? Has the time come to move away or to move home?

There is at least one other set of questions—the *who* questions.

"We make the journey inward," wrote Elizabeth O'Connor, "so that we can make the journey outward."

Our search for our calling leads us to listen deep within ourselves, hoping to hear the echo within, hoping to ungarble and understand the incarnate word spoken into us, hoping to discover how to live into and out of the echo of that word as it resounds within. But we are not meant to stay within ourselves forever. We are meant to be given away, to sound out our word in the world, to give it to others.

We are being given to others at all times. What else would being called be about? Our calling is about something considerably larger than our own fulfillment.

When we wrestle with our calling, part of what we are called to do is to see and hear and notice those to whom we in particular are being given.

We are called to make a jury box of sorts, called to take the time and to make the effort to discover who is being given to us and maybe to no one else. We are called to look for—and maybe even to find—a place and ways to serve where no one else will.

Who is knocking on your door these days? Who keeps calling?

Whose stories can you not get out of your mind and heart? Who keeps grinning when they see you coming? Who has a story that could be helped by hearing yours? Who could use a cup of cold water, and no one else has even noticed?

Who is my neighbor? Whose neighbors keep passing them by on the other side of the road?

To whom am I being given for this season of my life, for this stretch of my days? And who is being given to me? Who will go unnoticed or unattended if I do not answer this call?

"I have tried to write poetry for those for whom

there is no poetry," said the poet Philip Levine in a letter to a friend.

Who will have no poetry if I am not the poet?

Who will have no bread if I am not the baker? Who will see no light if I hide mine under a bushel?

To be called is to be sent. And we are being sent to someone as much as we are being sent by Someone.

To be called is to keep looking for those to whom we are being given.

six

Waiting

A man knows when he has found his vocation

when he stops thinking about how to live

and begins to live....

When we find our vocation—

thought and life are one.

—THOMAS MERTON

LAST FALL I WAS IN THE HILLS of northern Alabama. I was there to visit friends and to spend a week in one of my birthplaces.

The nice thing about being born again is that you get to have more than one birthplace.

I am up to about six. And that includes only the places where I think my work was born again. I was born again as a father when my younger children came to live with me after years of living in another house across town. I was born again in other ways too, as a husband, a friend, a pilgrim.

Born again is a phrase we hear sometimes from church folks. It is a way to talk about their spiritual life, and I understand that. *Born again* is also a way to describe what happens when something begins to shape us in a new way.

———

One of the birthplaces for my work was the family publishing business, the first place I learned anything about the world of work and the place where I learned of the possibility of making a living making art.

But when I was in my thirties, I was born again, again, in Chicago of all places.

A friend took me into his small consulting and marketing firm. That is where I learned to write sentences for pay.

Day after day, week after week, I would write everything from advertising to brochures to corporate communications to publicity materials to direct-mail solicitation. Day after day there would be a blank page and some instruction about what had to be put there, and at the end of every day, there would be hundreds of words that tried to accomplish the task.

I worked for a while for my friend in Chicago and then moved home to Nashville to try to do the same work on my own. I left my Chicago friend sort of quickly, clearly demonstrating that with everything he had given me a chance to learn, I had not learned as much as he knew about being a friend.

Over the next ten years, I learned how to find clients and land contracts. I learned how to buy photography and work with art directors. I learned to make enough of a living to have partners and employees and my name on the door.

I learned how to make a living with a pen in my hand. And I began to learn how to write. And I hope I learned, too, about being a friend.

However, I was not much of a businessman, and in a few years that became apparent. As I mentioned before, I nearly went bankrupt, and I did get divorced. I ended up in a psych ward. I lost most everything I owned. I also ended up being found by a crowd of new friends, who have turned out to be the finest ones I have ever known.

I also began to sense that after years of wrestling words on paper to nurture someone's business, I was ready to wrestle with words that might nurture someone's spirit.

———

That is how I ended up working for the Methodists. They needed someone who had worked in a commercial publishing house and could wield an editor's pencil. What I needed was for someone to take me in, and they were kind enough to do so.

They made it possible for me to earn a steady paycheck. They made it possible for me to go to the Academy, the place where my work and my prayer began to become one with each other. The Academy was the place where I began to listen more fiercely for and hear more clearly the echo within.

Those were the days in which I was introduced to the history and the habits of the ancient ways of prayer—disciplines and practices and traditions that had never been mentioned to me at all. I began to learn about paying attention for and seeing the Holy in the world in ways I had never been taught, even after nearly forty years of hanging around religious folks. I began reading the saints and praying the Liturgy of the Hours. I began studying the Rule of Saint Benedict, trying to take monastic wisdom and practice and to transpose some of each into my own life.

Something about those ancient traditions began to resonate with something deep within me.

As the sun set each day at the Academy, we would gather to say evening prayer and to take the Eucharist. There was always a sermon or a homily at evening prayer. *Sermon* is what they called it when a preacher did it, and we had a lot of clergy in our Academy. *Homily* is what they called it when one of us lay folks did it. The responsibility was passed around so that just about everyone in the community would have a chance to give one or the other during the two years.

My turn was to come during the next to last week we would gather as an Academy. At the time the schedule was drawn up, no one knew that the Thursday homilist for the May session of our Academy was going to spend much of his April in a psych ward. Including the homilist himself.

On an evening in May, in a particular year of our Lord I will forever regard as a Year of Jubilee, in the chapel at an old Methodist campground in what passes for mountains in northern Alabama, I read an original story that passed for a homily to a crowd of folks at the Academy.

And I went from being a wordsmith to being a writer. It was like being born again, again.

———

By then I had been working for pay for more than twenty years. And most of that time and labor had been spent simply trying to sell something to someone or for someone. I was happy to have been paid to learn to be a wordsmith. I was treated nicely by the clients and companies for whom I worked. I was not embarrassed about doing such commercial work with my art.

But as time had gone by, I had begun to hear something within that said to me it was time for different work than the work I was doing.

"I did not want to write for pay," wrote Leonard Cohen. "I wanted to be paid for what I wrote."

"The painting...did not tell a story," says Artemisia in a novel by Susan Vreeland. "I had gotten paid for craft, not for art."

I remember where I was sitting when I read those sentences. I remember the yes that echoed within.

Our callings are revealed to us in different ways.

There are people who are naturals of one sort or another. They seem born to do this one thing or that one, and they walk right into it and never look back. There is never any doubt in their mind or any detour in their journey.

Other people work for a while, and then something happens. There is a moment of clarity for them, and they suddenly see what they are on the planet to do, and they go and do it.

Still others of us do one thing for a while and then another. We keep showing up, drawn to the work we are given to do. Over time the practice of the craft, the time spent, the pace and the joy and the struggle shape us and change us.

For most of us, finding our calling involves some combination of the above.

In time, I went from being a publisher to being an adman—a wordsmith, if you will. Not exactly a businessman and not exactly an artist, but I was writing every day, writing for a living. I was no longer the same. I had been born again.

Then I went from being an adman to an editor, a different kind of wordsmith. I was learning the craft of writing books. I was not yet an artist, not yet a writer, but I was closer to art than I was to business.

In time, the echo of the incarnate word whispered into me, the word that gave birth to Robert in the first place, gave birth to a writer.

———

I have not told the tale of even half of my birthplaces.

If I was born again at the family business and in the four-person creative shop in downtown Chicago, then I was born again working for the Methodists and in a small room where I ghostwrote a book and learned I could actually write one.

I was born again as well in the pew and at the altar of a church on Woodland Street and another on West End and another on Broadway in our town.

I was born again when the lady to whom I am married said yes and again when two of my children came to live with us.

I was born again on the day a telephone call came and with it the news that someone wanted to publish my first book, the one with that story I had given as a homily in Alabama. I danced and laughed and cried my way around the yard until the neighbors came to see if I was okay. And I was.

I was born again one day watching the sun come up out of the sea and realizing the notion for a book had come up with the sun. And another day on my knees in the backyard digging holes for roses and finding another set of stories had begun to grow.

Sometimes it seems we have birthplaces all over the place.

seven

Living

Jesus lived the ordinary life
of the men of His time,
in order to sanctify the ordinary lives
of men of all time.
If we want to be spiritual, then,
let us first of all live our lives.

—THOMAS MERTON

IN A CHURCH WHERE I WAS SPEAKING the other day, a young man introduced me. Two or three things he said caught my attention.

The first was that he referred to me as one of his mentors. *Why can we not just be friends?* I thought to myself. One of the disadvantages of being old enough to be his father is that the age gap may have suggested to him that we cannot be friends because we are not contemporaries. I am honored someone thinks I know something worth hearing or thinking about, but I am hesitant to give up the notion I am still a young man myself.

I do wish I knew half as much as he evidently thinks I might. Another disadvantage of my age is that I know me well enough to know I cannot possibly live up to his expectations. He is a kind young man, and I am sure he would cut a friend some slack. I do not know whether or not he will be as merciful to a mentor.

There is a well-known songwriter in this town whom I have admired for a long time. I introduced my children to his albums when they were young. Most people would not have heard his records; most people who have heard of him know him only by his songs, songs made famous by other people's recordings of them. The writer in me has always appreciated his craftsmanship.

I saw him one day sitting on a bench in a park. And I could not resist shaking his hand.

"You do not know me, but my children and I have listened to your records for years and have always enjoyed them and admired your work. My kids would think less of me if I got this close and did not say thank you."

He looked at me with a twinkle in his eye. "Well," he said, "I question your judgment, but I do appreciate your support."

I thought of the songwriter when my young friend introduced me as his mentor.

———

The introduction went on for another couple of minutes. It went on long enough for me to check my pulse to be sure I was being introduced and not eulogized.

Then he looked in my direction and said, "And I want his life."

I knew what he meant, so I smiled back at him. But in my head I said, *Not so fast, buddy. This is my life, and you cannot have it. Get your own.*

He and I have talked about this before. He is listening fiercely to the echo within himself these days, and he is beginning to imagine certain specifics of the life to which he believes he is being called. He wants to write, and he wants to not have a day job, and he wants to have a studio in his back garden. He wants to find folks who will be kind enough to publish his sentences, and he wants to have an audience who will be gracious enough to read them.

I know that he is young and has a lot of choices in front of him. He will be drawn to different things as time goes by, and he will hear different parts of the echo within. Perhaps some or all of those things he dreams of now will make up the life to which he is being called. I do not know.

I do know we have talked enough about what he has heard so far of the echo within to know what he meant when he said he wanted my life.

He still cannot have it.

———

When I was young, I did not want to grow up to be like my father. I wanted to grow up to be my father.

He was gentle and wise and funny. He was a visionary publisher, a fine writer, a great speaker, and an above-average teller of jokes.

People grinned when they saw him coming, whether they were employees at the family company, artists or writers with whom he worked in the business, people who read his books or went to hear him speak, or college students in the class he taught at church.

The people who grinned at him the biggest were the people who lived in the same house with him. We all adored him, even when we were angry with him about the sorts of things that anger people when seven of them with the same last name live under the same roof.

For years the arc of the story of the life I believed I would live was right in front of me.

I was going to graduate from the college where my father and grandfather went. I was going to marry a girl from the church and have a big family. Then I was going to become a beloved member of the church we Bensons had been attending for four generations. Being beloved meant teaching a class and serving on the board and filling in at the pulpit from time to time, just like my father.

I was going to be a legendary publisher my own self.

I did not have a piece of land picked out for my big house along the river, but I knew whose house would be just down the road.

There was plenty of clear evidence that being my father would be a good thing to be. And who better than his first son, his namesake no less, might God call to be the next Bob Benson?

———

I spend a fair amount of time around writers and publishers and literary agents and such.

More than once I have heard writers, most often new writers, ones not yet published, describe their new book. They will say something like, "You know, like so-and-so's work."

And more than once I have heard a literary agent who is a friend of mine mutter, "Don't bother. We already have a so-and-so."

Then she'd pause and say to the writer, "Be yourself."

That is part of what it means to discover one's calling. The world already had a Bob Benson. There was not going to be another one. Or if there was, it was not going to be me.

Most everything about my life is on a smaller scale than my father's. Including the size of my family and the square footage of my house. By almost any measurement—acreage or legend or influence—I clearly did not turn out to be Bob Benson.

I did enroll in the college my father went to. But I was only there a short time. It may have been his place, but it was not ever really meant to be mine.

My time in the family business revealed I had precious few of the skills and the instincts needed. I had trouble rising to the level of usefulness, let alone legend.

Until I was in my twenties, I went to the big church where all those generations of Bensons had gone. But then I fell in love with the art of the liturgical church—all of the smells and bells and chants and such. I discovered that not only is it difficult to go home again; sometimes you cannot go to your old church again either.

"Life is what happens while you are making other plans," observed John Lennon.

Living is very often what happens when we think we have God's plan for our lives all mapped out. The choices we make, the curves we are thrown, the chances we take, the hunches we follow are all part of our mysterious journey in the direction of who we were whispered into being to become.

I made what seemed the right choice for college and ended up not being able to fit in there and never being comfortable at college anywhere and so never finishing. I could not handle the curves that came with being married so young, and the shape of my relationships with my children was affected for my whole life. I took a chance on a friend in Chicago and ended up learning the craft to which I have been drawn since I was a boy. I played a hunch and went to work at the

Upper Room and stumbled into my life's work. A life's work that seemed like an old friend when the time finally came to do it.

I spent a lot of years hearing and responding to what I believed then and believe even now were different callings on and in and around and into my life. The length of the journey and its twists and turns were not a function of my not properly hearing the echo within; they were a function of my living the life I was given at the time, the life I was spoken into being to live.

———

I know what my friend means when he says he wants my life. At least I know what it means to feel that way about the life of someone you admire. I am the man who grew up wanting to be the next Bob Benson.

I am flattered that my young friend aspires to some of the things I aspire to and that he holds dear some of the things I hold dear. I am honored that he uses me for a model. Though I do question his judgment.

The fact that he finds things in my living out my echo within that resonate with what he is hearing is a grace and a gift to us both. But he cannot be Robert. For better or for worse, we already have one of those.

What we do not have yet is whoever he was whispered into being to be. That is the life for which only he was spoken into being in the first place. He is the only one who can ever hear that incarnate word, the only one who will ever have a real clue as to what that echo is saying to him and where it is calling him.

That is the life to which he is being called. He must become his word, not someone else's.

eight

Knowing

There is a stage in the spiritual life
in which we find God in ourselves—
this presence is a created effect of His love.
It is a gift of His, to us.

—THOMAS MERTON

SOMETHING INTERVENES and changes everything—makes everything possible, rearranges the board, shifts the landscape, or whatever phrase you want to use—and a door opens or a series of doors, and you are staring your life's work in the face. Or your vocation is staring at you.

Sometimes you know when it happens. But sometimes years and years go by before you begin to see it for what it is.

Sometimes someone has to explain to you what seems to be taking place as events unfold, lest you completely miss their significance.

The echo within can only be heard by the one into whom that particular incarnate word of God was spoken, but sometimes others can help us listen for what they themselves will never hear.

Which is partly what happened to me.

———

My father was a young man when he died. I know he was young; he was the age I am as I write this.

But to this day he occupies a tremendous place in my life. I know I am not the only son or daughter for whom such an occupation continues—this being under the influence of a parent who has long been gone.

My best friend, the woman to whom I am married and the person on the planet who knows me best, once said to me that there is a sense in which my vocation began when my father died—and maybe could not have begun until he did. I was taken aback when she made her observation. But I have come to believe she is right.

I do not mean that God took my father home so Robert could become a writer. The God of all wisdom would have made a better trade than that. In fact, if God wants to go that far, I am still willing to play second base for the Yankees.

But I do believe I so loved and admired my father and the stories he put on paper and the talks he made in front of crowds that I might never have attempted either one for fear of being forever not as good. I might never have been willing to show my work to publishers for fear of riding on my father's coattails.

There is a chance that were he alive—something more precious to me than writing my own books—I would perpetually be Bob's boy in a lot of ways and in a lot of places and even now would still be trying to figure out how to become Robert.

———

My father had been ill off and on for fifteen years, suffering from cancer. All of us who loved him carried with us the knowledge there would come a day when the doctors could not get to the recurring cancer with a knife, and the time finally came.

The family was together at Christmas, and then he and my mother went south to take a cruise for a week. He got off the boat and caught a plane home to Nashville. He got off the plane and went straight to the hospital. That was in January. He came home once for two days and one night but had to go back in almost immediately.

He died in his sleep, and in ours, early one morning in the dark, toward the end of March.

In the last few weeks before he died, the doctors made him comfortable enough to spend a certain amount of each day sitting up in bed and saying good-bye to folks.

They came from all over, writers and poets and singers and publishers and preachers and friends—folks who had fallen into step with him along the way and for whom he had been mentor and poet and friend and fellow pilgrim. They would call to figure out which day would work best to come to town. We would meet them in the waiting room and take them up to have a few minutes with him so he could say good-bye to them.

Some months later, talking to one of his friends about those days, I realized he never said good-bye to me.

A long time passed before I would admit it to myself or tell anyone else, but I felt horribly left out and unfairly treated.

I worked beside him in the yard most every weekend when I was growing up. He loved to garden; I just loved being beside him. (I did not mind the allowance and the use of the car on Friday night either, I suppose.)

I traveled a lot of miles with him while he went around the country learning to be the gifted speaker he became. I worked with him in the family business for years and sat in countless halls and airports and dressing rooms with him. I edited books for him, helped negotiate his contracts, booked appearances for him. We shared late-night telephone calls, reading things to each other. Together we wrestled with wrestling with words for years.

I knew things about him that few others knew. I

knew that when he was young, he dreamed of writing novels about the Royal Canadian Mounted Police. I knew he was a P. E. teacher once and drove a school bus and sold vacuum cleaners door to door. I knew he liked butter-pecan ice cream, corn cakes rather than pancakes, and sliced tomatoes with every meal when they were in season.

I knew he always said that the reason he had been a poor pastor when he was young was that every time he had a membership drive, he drove off half the membership.

I also knew that in those last few years he was drawn to the ancient traditions of the church that had not been a part of his experience. I saw the way writers from more liturgical traditions began to deepen and shape him. I watched as more contemplative practice began to draw him into new ways of finding and being found by the One Who spoke him into being.

I was even the guy who handled the "come and say good-bye to Bob Benson" schedule for him and all of his friends in those last few days.

And in the end, he did not even say good-bye to me.

———

It took a while for me to absorb the notion of having been left out of the good-bye round. Another little while went by before I could talk about it. Like ten years.

I am slow about some things.

I finally told the story to my wise friend Ben. I do not see him often, once a year in a good year. Almost every time I see him, some bit of his wisdom or his insight or his direction changes me and the way I live my life. I saw him three years in a row once, and everything in my life changed so much that I was forced to stay away from him for a couple of years so my head could stop spinning.

"He did not even say good-bye to me," I said to Ben. "Me. Of all people."

Ben looked past me for a while, a mannerism which means he is thinking. Or at least it means he knows how to look like he is thinking. Whichever is the case, I have learned to be still and silent and wait to hear what Ben is about to say.

"He knew that you knew," Ben said. And then he went back to looking past me for another while.

In a few minutes he started up again. "Your father did not need to say good-bye to you in order to tell you that he hated to leave you. He knew that you knew that.

"And he did not need to say good-bye to you to make sure you heard something from him he had never had a chance to say to you.

"He knew that you knew. He knew you knew everything he knew to tell you—as a father, as a friend, as a poet, and as a pilgrim."

———

My father taught me that a writer has three jobs.

The first job is to learn the craft. No matter how much talent you hit the ground with, if you want to get very far, you are going to have to work at the craft. You are going to have to practice every day, you are going to have to read good stuff until you know good from bad, and you are going to have to learn how to write sentences that people want to read, sentences that make them want to read the next one as well.

You begin to learn the craft as soon as you are willing to start doing the hard work required. And as soon as you can find a place or an audience or a context within which people begin to see your work and decide whether or not they want to finish the page or pay the fee.

The second job is to find your own voice. It is not always an easy thing to separate yourself from the voices you love. Even now, I have favorite writers I do not read while I am writing something new. Listening to their voices can make it harder for me to hear and hold true to and trust my own voice.

Early on, my father's voice—the voice of the writer I wanted to be—got in the way. I found my voice only after he had lost his altogether.

The last of the writer's three jobs is to figure out what you have to say and begin to say it. Most writers have only one or two things to say. We keep saying it in as many ways as we can, hoping we are finally saying it clearly enough that others begin to hear us.

"Write as if you were dying," writes Annie Dillard. "At the same time, assume you write for an audience consisting solely of terminal patients. That is, after all, the case....

"What could you say to a dying person that would not enrage by its triviality?" she goes on.

(The loud click you just heard is the sound of all of us who write putting down our pens at the same time.)

Discovering what matters most to you, much less what you might have to say about it, may take a while.

Another while may go by before you develop the nerve required to impose on the time of someone who is dying.

I do not believe that the advice from my father and from Ms. Dillard is just for writers. Or even just for artists of one sort or another.

Whatever work you do, whatever your calling, whatever are the specific details of living out the incarnate word spoken into you — the details you must work out with fear and trembling — their advice is still sound.

Whatever our craft, we are called to do our work "in truth and beauty and for the common good," as the old prayer says. A doctor or a draftsman, a preacher or a plumber, a shopkeeper or a saleswoman — anyone for that matter — would do well to practice hard at the craft required to do the work to which they have been given. Whatever gifts and graces and talents were spoken into us should be respected and nurtured.

One's voice is another word for one's essence, in a way, another way to think about what we bring to our work that is a reflection of the incarnate word within us. And what particular gifts and instincts and perspectives and insights that only we have to offer to the people for whom we do it.

I also believe that the work we do is better when we know why it matters, to us or to anyone else. Such work is more fulfilling and its fruit more rewarding. Work that grows out of what matters to us the most is the work that does the most good for those for whom it is done.

I grew up knowing these things, without knowing that I knew them.

Which is why I am glad for the wisdom of my two friends—the sweet woman with whom I share my life and my friend I see once a year or so. Because they were right, both of them.

I did know the things my father wanted me to know. It just took me a while to discover that I knew them.

And in the discovery I finally stumbled on how to become Robert, on how to take the echo of the Voice within and its call upon me and turn some bit of that echo into my own voice and my own work. And finally into Robert.

A Robert who is happy to have been Bob's boy.

nine

Choosing

When the right time comes
for us to go on to other things,
God withdraws the sense of His presence,
in order to strengthen our faith....
The time has come
when we must go out of ourselves
and above ourselves
and find Him no longer within us
but outside us and above us.

—THOMAS MERTON

I LIKE MY DUCKS IN A ROW. I like my t's crossed and my i's dotted. I like, as the old revival song says, my old accounts to be settled. I like for things to go the way we drew them up on the blackboard, to go according to plan, to be right on the money.

These are things I have to be careful about when I am trying to listen for the calling voice of God. God does not seem to be particularly interested in whether or not my ducks stay in line.

I do not think I am the only one for whom this is true. The story of the twelve disciples comes to mind.

We who gather in churches spend a fair amount of time telling each other the story of Jesus and His disciples. After all of these years of storytelling, two thousand or so of them, we have come to see these men as saints. Rightly so, by my lights. But before they were a crowd of saints, they were a crowd of average guys, as near as we can tell. Our information about them is sketchy, and *sketchy* is generous.

Some of them were fishermen. Probably their fathers had been fishermen too. They had boats and nets and places on the beach and regular customers.

There was the one tax collector, whose profession did not exactly make him a favorite among the locals, but everyone has to earn a living, and someone had to earn a living collecting taxes. There was the one physician.

Who knows what the rest of them did?

All of them, though, had work to do and places to be. They had customers to take care of and business to do and houses to maintain. They probably had seats at the synagogue and wives and children and in-laws and neighbors.

They had a favorite pub and a favorite team and a favorite shirt, I suppose.

And they had dreams and hopes and prayers. They had promises they had made and promises they had been given. And they had a sacred Story too, one that the Hebrew people had told each other for centuries, one they likely understood no better than we understand the sacred Story we Christians tell each other all these years later.

Their story told them to watch for the coming of Immanuel, God With Us. Our story calls Him Jesus. He is the One Who said to them, "Follow Me," and this crowd of average guys said yes, and nothing was the same ever again.

After that, there were nets to leave behind and multitudes to feed. There were dinners with publicans and sinners, and there was trouble with the authorities. There was a drama at Mary and Martha's house, and there was the upper room and the feast and the cross and the fear. There was the resurrection, and there was the being left alone. There was the church to build and missionary journeys to saddle up for and a community to gather up and a new Story to tell. Or a new way to tell the Story they had always known.

All along there was a sort of daily saying yes to the whole thing. And there was also the occasional yes that had to be said to a larger thing, a thing that was farfetched at best and crazy at worst.

I wonder if they noticed the moment of the saying yes to traveling along with each other. The fisherman and the tax collector. The brothers and the friends, the ones who betrayed and denied the One Who came among them, the ones who ran away, the doubters and the unknown ones. I wonder sometimes if they kept up with each other.

———

There is a sense in which our being called and our saying yes to that calling can be seen as actions that essentially affect us as individuals. It is the echo within each of us, and only within each of us as individuals, to which we respond. No one else can hear what echoes within us.

It is also true that our response to that echo, our yes, always leads us to others. Some of them are jury-box sort of folks, the ones to whom we have been given and who have been given to us, the ones for whom our work is done. They go by other names—audience, congregation, class, patients, constituency, customers, students, and the list goes on to include whatever name we use for such a group in our lives.

It is also true that our yes leads us to another crowd of others, the ones we walk beside for a season or two or seventeen. They are the people we call friend or neighbor or co-worker. They are the people who enter our lives because we said yes.

———

We sort of wander along, sometimes feeling alone and in the dark, and then comes an Invitation to follow. Some new thing resonates with the echo within, and it is time to rearrange the ducks or gather them up from the places to which they have scattered. In the doing of it, we discover we are surrounded by new faces; we discover we have been given to some new people, or at least people who are new to us.

Which does not mean we will never feel as though we are wandering in the dark again, but we are reminded that if we pay attention, we will rarely be left alone. Which is no mere thing.

———

The last major rearrangement of the ducks in my life came a few years ago when my two youngest children came to live with us.

I cannot tell the whole story here or perhaps anywhere ever; some of it is not even mine to tell. I cannot begin to tell you about all of the joys and the wonders, the good days and the not-so-good ones, the treats and the tricks that came with the four of us saying yes to each other. Someday I may be poet enough to say what the richness of those years together means to me.

But I do have at least two observations to make. One is that calling is not always only about who we are or what we do. It is not always strictly about our work. Sometimes it is about who is beside us. And who we are beside.

When the children came, we moved across town from a suburban neighborhood where we knew precious few of our neighbors, to be sure, and into a little neighborhood where people walk the sidewalks and sit on their porches. Most of my friends whom I had ever had before had been connected to the work I do. My friends were writers and publishers, editors and agents, and the media folks and sales folks whose hard work made it possible for the rest of us to make a living.

I did not know many schoolteachers or human resource people, radio correspondents or accountants. I did not know any fishermen or tax collectors or publicans, for that matter.

Because of one yes almost ten years ago now, a yes said to an invitation that had nothing to do with making new friends, I have all these new friends in my life these days, people who walk along beside me and mine.

There are the two couples down the street who bring their young children to swim in our pool. There is the couple at the corner who watches our house while we travel. There is a friend who used to stay with the children when we had to be away on business, when my children were still here.

There are coaches and teachers, landscapers and translators, radio folks and number crunchers. There is a whole world of people I would never have known, and my life would be the poorer for it.

The list is longer, much longer. For a shy person, a person who has spent most of his life as other, I have a huge list of people who walk beside me every day.

We may well travel along together until my traveling days are done. We may well go in and out of one another's lives and days and schedules and houses and backyards for the rest of my time.

We may also break one another's hearts. Not because of a dark or clumsy thing one of us does to the other, though it can happen, but likely because someone will get a better job and move to another town. Someone else will need a bigger house and have to leave the neighborhood. They will promise to visit, but they will not.

Callings can change. They can shift and grow, expand and contract, mirroring and responding to the choices we make as we seek to live out the details of the echo within that we can hear.

And when they do, we can find ourselves walking alongside people we never expected to see. And we can find ourselves walking along without someone we had come to count on.

———

Twelve months and two weeks ago I was about to get on a plane and head off to Carolina to spend the weekend with a crowd of church folks who had become good friends of mine.

I had been lucky enough to meet one of the pastors at another conference. She heard me speak there and asked if I could come to their church sometime. I told her what I usually tell folks—that I will go anywhere to listen to myself talk—so they invited me. I went back there for some years in a row, about the same time each year. I became, as astonishing as it seemed to me then and as astonishing as it still is now, a sort of poet-in-residence for them. Even though I was only in residence for one weekend a year.

This year the woman who had invited me is no longer there. In fact, the whole staff has changed. I do not think it was my fault. I am friends with the district superintendent, and I could call and ask, but I am afraid to. I want to believe it just had to do with the way things change in churches.

Which is, I suppose, the way things change every-where else too. Even in our own lives.

———

Sometimes what we want is to be allowed to hunker down in the life we are living, or are hoping to live, or are constructing for ourselves. Without any upset, without any change in plans, without any of our ducks being disturbed.

But sometimes when we say yes to some new thing that seems to be calling to us from the echo within, then we may as well be prepared to head for God knows where after that. And to head there with God knows who as well.

Any attempt—no matter how clumsy or cautious, no matter how courageous or clever—to live out what one thinks one hears in the calling voice of God within must be lived out in the face of change.

Our companions will change; our journeys will take us in and out of relationships. Promises will be made, and promises will be broken. And so will our hearts.

The only way to avoid it is to not say yes.

ten

Dreaming

The things that we love
tell us what we are.

—THOMAS MERTON

ON THE WAY TO SOMEWHERE I sat next to a man on a plane. He had all the accouterment of a businessman—briefcase, business suit, and a pile of reports. He had a mobile telephone he talked on ceaselessly until the plane took off, played games on after we got in the air, and announced his arrival on when we landed. He also had a laptop and an iPod and a *Wall Street Journal.* We do not see many of those guys on Southwest Airlines.

We had the sort of scintillating conversation you get when you are a stranger and you happen to sit next to me.

"Excuse me, is that seat taken?" That is my clever ice-breaking line when I have to get over to the window seat. Pretty good, huh?

Later I said, "Do you mind if I put the shade down?" Brilliant conversationalist. When the category is small talk, mine almost always qualifies.

I am not a big talker on airplanes. If you talk too much, you have a hard time keeping your teeth clenched in fear. I mostly scribble in my sketchbook while I am hurtling through the air in a large machine that has no business being this far off the ground. The man made a couple of attempts to talk to me, but I was up to the task of avoiding conversation, and he was forced to talk to a man across the aisle.

Just as the time came for us to stand in the aisle and wait our turn to get off the plane, he asked me a question. He cleverly deduced this was his last chance to make me make conversation. He chose that moment when I am generally saying to myself that people with actual luggage in the overhead bins should be forced to sit in their seats until those of us who do not have actual luggage in the overhead bins can get off the plane first since we clearly and considerately packed more efficiently than they. The recent announcement by many airlines that all of us will have to pay to check our bags means I am going to have to find something else to feel superior about when I fly.

"What do you do?" he asked.

Something about my beard and my ponytail, my eyeglasses in a style most commonly associated with the folks who led the Russian Revolution, my lack of socks with my loafers even though January had just begun, the bush jacket, the purse, and the sketchbook had suggested to him that perhaps I was not a businessman. I could see how he had become a captain of industry.

"I am a writer," I said.

He got this grin on his face. "I knew you were a something," he said triumphantly.

———

People very often think that all sorts of artists are at least different, if not something.

If you close your eyes and think about it, though I cannot imagine why you would before this moment when I have tricked you into doing so, you can see me in my one-room studio at the back of my garden. Just sort of operating in this dreamlike state, looking like a writer, living the writer's life.

Surrounded by my books, hunched over an antique desk, cardigan and beret and pipe and fountain pen. Seemingly always lost in or on the edge of a divine and mystical state, poised to snatch a deep truth out of the air and out of my heart, then scribbling quickly to be sure some marvelous thing has been captured for our collective edification and wonder.

I know, I know, I never think of me like that either. But it is a good dream, is it not? If not for you, most certainly for me.

I was thirteen when I first dreamed such a dream. Or perhaps when the dream first dreamed me.

———

Long before he became well known for the other things he became, my father was known as a poet. His first published work was a series of poems that ran as a newspaper column, and his first book was a collection of some of those poems.

He brought home books by other poets as well. I do not know if my father intended for me to, but at some point when I was young, I started picking up the books and reading them.

Before long I had begun to scribble things of my own. And before too much longer, *poet* was the word I used to describe what was echoing in me, what I thought I might become when I grew up.

———

By then I was a freshman in high school, and I had fallen way under the influence of Paul Simon. Or as far as one could fall by listening to the same two albums over and over and over again.

I began to take his lyrics—which I knew by heart after a few weeks—and rewrite them to tell the story of what was in my heart instead of his.

The importance of the exercise had less to do with vocation and more to do with the fact that I thought I had an audience already, an audience of one. And if I could dazzle her with original love poems, she might even notice me.

I spent the better part of algebra classes rewriting Mr. Simon's lyrics (the only thing this poet ever found algebra classes good for, by the way). These poems were going to be the key to my having a steady girlfriend. And in the days in which I grew up, going steady mattered.

Having spent the better part of a decade hanging around school kids while mine went through middle and then high school, I have noticed that these days kids are not so quick to pair off as they were when I was young. Psychologists and sociologists may well be able to demonstrate that such behavior is a good thing; I do not know. But I worry whether or not they have enough bad love poetry in their lives.

One day my father brought home a couple of books by Rod McKuen, a poet who was popular at the time. I always had the impression there were a fair number of critics and other poets who thought his work was too commercial, too sweet and sappy. They may have been right, though it did not matter much to me at the time and does not even now. I have to confess that on the few occasions I mentioned him to writers over the years, they sort of giggled me into never mentioning him again.

What mattered to me was that when I read his poems, they made me want to write my own.

These were also the years when I was introduced to Thoreau, who advised me to advance confidently in the direction of my dreams, and I believed him.

I suppose the people who introduced me to Mr. Thoreau and Mr. Simon and Mr. McKuen may have expected me to dream of being a contributing member of society. I dreamt of being a poet instead.

I grew up to carry sketchbooks instead of briefcases and travel without any reports to read on the plane.

Mr. McKuen came to town once to perform. He read his poems against the backdrop of an orchestra.

My father took me to hear him. The concert was in the old Ryman Auditorium, the best concert hall in our town at the time.

There was going to be Porter Wagoner and Dolly Parton and Ernest Tubb on stage on Saturday night, but on this evening during the week, there was going to be a poet. A poet from New York and lately San Francisco no less, no small thing for a Nashville kid in the sixties.

Mr. McKuen knew his way around a stage and an audience because he had started out as a singer. He had ruined his vocal cords along the way, which is why he turned to writing poetry instead. His reading voice was a scratchy, broken, whispery sort of thing that made you want to keep clearing your throat to help him with his. He joked that he sounded as though he had been gargling with Drano.

He read his poems, and he told his stories about how they came to be, how and where he wrote, and what life was like for the poet he had stumbled into becoming.

When the concert was over, my father and I worked our way through the crowd and out the door toward our car. We headed across the street. As we walked across the parking lot, I could see the front door of my father's office. I did not notice on that night the circular nature of the walk we were taking, but I am aware of it now. We were walking the same sidewalk we had walked a few years before on the day I went to the Christmas party at my father's office and began to fall in love with words on paper.

I did not make the connection that night. That night I was only thinking, *Mr. McKuen looked like a poet, and he acted like a poet, and he talked like a poet.*

And I knew I wanted to be one.

If I had been poet enough then, I would have gone home and written about the echo within.

———

Years later, on the first day of the Academy, a man stood up to welcome us all.

"Everything in your life," he said that day, "every song, every story, every prayer, every person you have ever known—everything in your life has conspired to bring you to this very moment in this very place for this very thing."

When I listen to my life, as Mr. Buechner suggested, I can name more and more of the moments when I could hear the echo of the incarnate word that was whispered into me.

———

Can we become something or another simply by dreaming it and believing in the dream hard enough and long enough?

There is some evidence one can do just that. I am not the only one who has wandered into living the sort of life and doing the sort of work I have always dreamed of. And it did not happen to me because I am particularly smart or driven or even gifted.

Does the fact that we dream of being this or that and believe in the dream so strongly mean that we have heard our calling, that this is the thing the One Who spoke us into being in the first place saw us becoming and doing and being?

I cannot say for sure, but I can say this: What better place to hide the mystery of who we are to become than within our own selves? How far-fetched would that be for a God who, according to Saint Paul, hid the secret to the whole world in us?

Can it be that one is somehow less, or one's sense of vocation and calling is somehow less, because one did not have a clear sense of the echo within so early? No, of course not.

A vocation found at the end of a long and twisting and surprising journey is no less a vocation than a vocation hoped for and dreamed of and lived for a lifetime. A vocation stumbled into is no less a vocation either.

To assume the One Who made us has only one way of revealing to us the thing for which we were made is to attempt to handcuff the Almighty. (Something neither advisable or—I suspect—possible.)

We dream a dream, and it does not easily come true, and we conclude that perhaps it was not what God meant for us after all. But I suspect far too many of us give up on our dreams far too soon.

We get impatient, and we get frustrated. We get discouraged, and we get beaten about in the way that life does sometimes. We get dug in with mortgages and car payments to make and houses to keep up and children to feed. We get on a career path, and we cannot find a rest area, much less an exit.

And sometimes another thing happens. Sometimes we are nudged a bit at a time in the direction of our dreams even though it is not clear to us for years and years.

Guess Who is doing the nudging?

———

I am aware that my story sounds like a direct line ran through the forty years between my visit to the office Christmas party and my daily work in the studio in the back garden where I scribble sentences these days.

The truth is, I did not feel as though I was on a direct line for hardly any moment of this journey. It did not appear that way to me at any point. Until now, oddly enough.

I went from poet to publisher to wordsmith to editor to writer, but it took a long time. I went from poetry to prose. I went from here to Chicago and back. I went from the Nazarenes to the Methodists to the Episcopalians. And from Paul Simon to James Taylor, who is now unofficially responsible for the official soundtrack for my life. Except for certain sacramental moments for which Johann Sebastian Bach is more particularly suited.

Whenever I was unsure whether or not the time had come to move or change, to pursue this work instead of that, to try my hand at one thing and then another, I learned that only one thing was certain to help—listening. Listening as fiercely as possible to see if what I was about to do next seemed to resonate with the echo within. Did it ring true? Did it sound like part of the word whispered into me by the One Who whispered me into being?

Over the years I went from an oddly dressed, introverted young man to an oddly dressed, introverted older man.

But according to the guy on the plane, I am a something—not a famous one or a well-known one or even one who gets to read his things with an orchestra. But I am the something I always dreamed of being.

Our journeys begin with a whisper, a word spoken by the One Who has spoken and is still speaking all things into being. We live in the hope of discovering and articulating and reflecting the incarnate word that echoes within. And in the hope of becoming the someone we were spoken into being to be.

A Few Notes

THERE ARE SOME THINGS I want you to know about some of the things in the book you just read. Or are about to read, depending on whether or not, like me, you always go to the back and read the author's notes first. I like to be in on any insider jokes as I go along.

The first thing to know is that I am grateful you are even taking the time to read my work. The purist in me says that I would write whether anyone read it or not, but it is much better to be read.

The second thing has to do with the quotations in the book.

The epigraphs throughout are taken from Thomas

Merton's *Thoughts in Solitude,* a book that is about far more than one hermit's contemplative life. I recommend it highly.

I also recommend the following, other books that I have read over and over and from whence came some of the other quotations—

The Writing Life / Annie Dillard

Now and Then / Frederick Buechner

Shaped by the Word / Robert Mulholland

Eighth Day of Creation / Elizabeth O'Connor

Letters to a Young Poet / Rainer Maria Rilke

The Passion of Artemisia / Susan Vreeland

I also found quotations in one of two anthologies of sorts, and I suggest you have a look at them as well— *The Hand of the Poet* by Rodney Phillips and *A Guide to Prayer for Ministers and Other Servants* by Rueben Job and Norman Shawchuck.

Any of the books can be found in whatever ways you go about hunting down good books. I know this because I am forever loaning my copies of these books to someone and having to replace them.

You should also know that all scriptures are the author's paraphrase. And that all the prayers are adapted from *The Book of Common Prayer of the Episcopal Church in America* (1979).

And that the Academy for Spiritual Formation is a part of the Upper Room in Nashville, Tennessee, and they would be happy to hear from you. Tell them Robert said hello.

The Rule of Saint Benedict was written in the sixth century to regulate the lives of the monks under Benedict's care. His rule has become the center point for Christian monastic life in the years since, regardless of the particular order of monks. My favorite translation of the rule is the Vintage Spiritual Classics edition, edited by Timothy Fry, O.S.B., and published by Random House.

———

One last note.

No one makes books by themselves, no matter what they say. My experience is that no one should even try.

Thank you to my friends at WaterBrook—especially Steve, Jeanette, Carol, Lori, and Carrie.

And thank you as always to Ms. Lil of Dorchester Lane, without whom I would still be trying to finish any book at all.

And thank you to Miss Jones of Merigold, without whom I might never have had a chance to try.

—

And thank you again, gentle reader, for taking the time.

Be in touch.

Namaste—

R. Benson

In Sunnyside on the Feast of Saint James, 2008

ROBERT BENSON LIVES AND WRITES in Nashville, Tennessee. He is always happy to get notes from fellow pilgrims and other folks who are paying attention to the world around them. He even looks forward to writing back and will actually do so.

Write to Robert at 1001 Halcyon Ave., Nashville, TN 37204. Or visit him online and learn about his other books, inquire about speaking engagements, and otherwise see what he is up to at www.robertbenson writer.com.